A HISTORY

— OF —

·WASHINGTON COUNTY,

MARYLAND,

FROM THE EARLIEST SETTLEMENTS TO THE PRESENT TIME

INCLUDING A

HISTORY OF HAGERSTOWN

BY THOMAS J. C. WILLIAMS

TO THIS IS ADDED A BIOGRAPHICAL RECORD OF REPRESENTATIVE FAMILIES
PREPARED FROM DATA OBTAINED FROM ORIGINAL
SOURCES OF INFORMATION

Illustrated

PUBLISHERS:
JOHN M. RUNK & L. R. TITSWORTH,
1906.

PREFATORY NOTES.

The author of this book was engaged in newspaper work in Hagerstown as Editor of THE HAGERSTOWN MAIL for about 17 years. He came into possession of numerous files of Hagerstown newspapers. From these this History is principally compiled. It is not intended to be a book of reference; it does not profess to be free from inaccuracies. The sources from which the incidents related have been taken are many of them fallable. That part which relates to the Civil War does not profess to be a military history and in the exciting times of the War, while Washington County was the scene of great events, there were doubtless thousands of happenings which I have not recorded. During a considerable period of the War the newspapers were suspended. I have made free use of documents and facts recorded in Scharff's History of Washington County which is now out of print and cannot be obtained. I have felt free to do this because I gave to Mr. Scharff a large amount of the material which he used. Samuel Kercheval's history, together with articles in the newspapers about the pioneers and Indian Warfare are the authorities used for the colonial period and the manner of life of the early settlers. These chronicles are written without taking any thought of the "dignity of history." Many incidents are recorded which appear to be trivial. But they give a better understanding of the character of our people. If I have failed to make this history interesting it is not because of lack of abundant material, for Washington County has been the scene of great events and the dwelling place of many famous and interesting men and women.

In all my work, which began many years ago, I have received the aid and sympathy of my former partner in publishing The Mail and my close personal friend for the third of a century, Edwin Bell, an actor in many of the scenes that I have described and one who as an Editor and a public spirited and patriotic citizen has contributed greatly to the advancement and prosperity of his native county.

T. J. C. W.

A work such as we are now pleased to present to our many patrons, in which we have collected and placed in permanent form the annals of an interesting section of Maryland, has two sources of value. One of these is its historic utility as a memorial of the progress and development of the community, from the earliest period with which we could become acquainted through family records and traditions to the present day. The preservation of these data affords the means of illustrating and confirming or correcting and amending extant histories, and supplies material for the compilation of future ones. The second source of value is the personal interest attaching to the biographical and genealogical records comprising our portion of this work, either as studies of life and character, or as memoirs of individuals connected with the reader as relatives or fellow citizens.

On both these accounts, a collection of biographical records is a useful contribution to current literature and a legacy to succeeding generations. Colonies of various nationalities and creeds peopled the territory now comprising Washington County; their descendants have taken an active part in national affairs, in war and in peace; and it will be strange indeed if their annals have not brought to view many scenes and revealed many facts well worthy being noted and remembered.

In the execution of this work no pains were spared to ensure the absolute truth upon which its value depends. The material comprising the History of Washington County, except the chapter relating to the churches, which was mostly contributed by ministers and competent writers, credit for which is given in the several notes, was compiled by T. J. C. Williams, whose statement precedes ours and is to the point. His production must prove to be a valuable addition to the library of every one who is fortunate enough to secure a copy and will be a lasting tribute to his memory.

The biographical sketches were gathered from the most trustworthy sources by careful note-takers. After being arranged by competent writers, and neatly type-written, these biographies were submitted by mail and otherwise, for correction and revision, which we hope was so thorough that few if any errors in facts, names or dates will be found in the complete work. Those who furnished the data are, therefore, responsible for its genuineness and authenticity. Great care was taken to have the sketches as free from error as possible, but we do not hold ourselves responsible for mistakes, as no charge was made for the insertion of any reading matter contained in the book.

Let the History and Biographical Record of Washington County, the first in the United States to be named after the "Father of Our Country," lie as a green wreath on the resting place of those pioneers, who, driven from their foreign homes by persecution, braved the sorrows of expatriation and the perils of the wilderness through single-hearted devotion to principle; and of those who came from motives which, if less heroic, were not less laudable, desiring as they did to find room and favoring circumstances for the growth and prosperity of their families.

The worth of the posterity of these early pioneers has been proved by the religious, educational and benevolent institutions that have sprung up within the borders of Washington County; by the public works in which many have taken a distinguished part; by their record of military service, and their no less valuable services as civilians; in brief, by the whole social fabric which they have reared, and which makes the land rescued by their forefathers from the wilderness a region of homes, cultured, peaceful and inviting.

In conclusion the publishers acknowledge their indebtedness for the sympathy of the press throughout Washington County, and especially to THE MAIL, for its unceasing and untiring efforts, both in its Job Department and Bindery, where this work was executed and perfected; to the ministers and other writers for their valuable contributions; and to those enterprising citizens who lent their support and encouragement to the enterprise, without which we could not have carried it to a final completion. Doubtless there will be disappointment among those who may have expected us to perpetuate their memories at our own expense, but no one is to blame but themselves, for they had ample opportunity We take pride in the belief that we have more than fulfilled the promises made in our prospectus, and feel that we will receive the approbation of every reasonably disposed patron.

RUNK & TITSWORTH,
PUBLISHERS.

CONTENTS OF VOLUME I.

CHAPTER I

THE record of events proposed in this narrative embraces a period of only about one hundred and seventy years from the first settlement of white people within the present boundaries of Washington County, to the present time; yet events have been so crowded into this brief era, that it has seen the thirteen colonies of white men battling in the wilds of the New World grow into a mighty nation. It has seen the population of the American States increase from less than two millions to forty-five times that number.

It has seen a greater development of the practical appliances of civilization than was witnessed in the preceding ten centuries. There are men now living within the limits of Washington County who were living when Fulton launched his steamboat in the waters of the Hudson river; who were 10 years of age when iron plows were unknown in the world, who were over 20 years of age when the first train of passenger cars made the trial trip on the Liverpool and Manchester road, who were over 30 when the leading scientists of the age proved that no vessel could carry enough coal to steam across the Atlantic; who had reached middle life when the first telegram flashed over the wires. The period of this history has seen territory of the European colonies and of the United States increase from a narrow strip lying between the Allegany Mountains on the west to the Atlantic ocean and from the northern limits of Massachusetts to the southern limits of Georgia, until it now stretches three thousand miles from ocean to ocean and from St. Lawrence to the Gulf.

Washington County has been the scene of many events in this onward march of civilization which well deserve to be held in remembrance. It has been the scene of many a bloody struggle with the original possessors of the soil who have now passed away from its borders leaving only remnants behind for archæologists to speculate upon. It has sent forth many men who have been conspicuous in the country's history or have helped to develop and people the far west. It was the scene of one of the mighty battles of the Civil War and in its soil repose the ashes of many thousands who fell on the bloody fields of Antietam and South Mountain.

When the first settlement was made in this beautiful valley in the year 1735 or thereabout, the eastern part of the State had been settled by Europeans for over a hundred years and Virginia and Massachusetts for a longer period—and yet the struggle with the fierce difficulties in which our ancestors had engaged had been so great that it had taken a century to penetrate seventy-five miles from the shores of the Chesapeake into a valley more fertile and salubrious than any which had been then settled. The splendid valley of the Genesee in Western New York was still a wilderness in the undisturbed possession of the Oneidas, waiting for a colony from Washington County, which went there more than a half century later. Of the great cities of America only New York, Philadelphia and Boston had any existence, Baltimore was not laid out. The site of Washington was still a swamp and a pine forest; those of Chicago and Cincinnati were unbroken solitudes. The great forests which covered the valley of the Ohio had scarcely been entered by the trapper and hunter. The outlying settlements were in constant danger from the incursions of the blood-thirsty Indian, and the flying settlers were sometimes pursued with tomahawk and scalping knife far within the bounds of the well settled country. Once within its history has Washington County suffered such an incursion that every white person within its bounds who escaped the tomahawk fled for protection and safety across the mountain which divided them from civilization.

Of the Indians who inhabited this fair valley when the hardy pioneers first built their cabins between its mountains, it is difficult for us who have never heard the war-whoop, or seen them ply the tomahawk in the dead hour of night by the light of burning homes, to form any correct idea. We may well doubt whether the men and women who have had this experience would concede to the red man the title of "the noble savage." If we may judge by the intense hatred with which the early settlers regarded him, pursued him, and waged a war of extermination against him, we may conclude that they did not regard him as the illustration of many of the virtues. There can be but little doubt that the red man who now infests the confines of our far Western States is a degenerate descendant of his ancestors; yet it is certain that the Indians most emulated the qualities of the wild animals after which they named themselves —the ferocity of the wolf, the cunning of the fox and the venom of the rattlesnake.

"The opinion which many careful and just-minded persons of our time have formed touching the Indian of whom the settlers in the border-land then stood in constant dread, is a singular mixture of truth and romance. Time and absence have softened all that is vile in his character and left in full relief all that is good and alluring. We are in no danger of being tomahawked. We are not terrified by his war whoop. An Indian in his war-paint and feathers is now much rarer show than a Bengal tiger or a white bear from the polar sea. Of the fifty millions of human beings scattered over the land, not five millions have ever in their lives looked upon an Indian. We are therefore much more disposed to pity than to hate. But, one hundred years ago, there were to be found, from Cape Ann to Georgia, few men who had not many times in their lives seen numbers of Indians, while thousands could be found scattered through every State, whose cattle had been driven off, and whose homes had been laid in ashes by the braves of the six nations, who had fought with them from behind trees and rocks, and carried the scars of wounds received in hand to hand encounters.

"The opinions which such men and women held of the noble red man was, we may be sure, very different from those current among the present generation, and formed on no better authority than the novels of Cooper, and the lives of such warriors as Red Jacket and Brant. * * He was essentially a child of nature and his character was precisely such as circumstances made it. His life was one long struggle for food. His daily food depended, not on the fertility of the soil or the abundance of the crops, but on the skill with which he used his bow; on the courage with which he fought, single-handed, the largest and fiercest of beasts; on the quickness with which he tracked, and the cunning with which he outwitted the most timid and keen-scented. His knowledge of the habits of animals surpassed that of Audubon. The shrewd devices with which he snared them would have elicited the applause of Ulysses; the clearness of his vision excelled that of the oldest sailor; the sharpness of his hearing was not equalled by that of the deer. While he underwent the most excruciating torture the ingenuity of his enemies could devise; while his ears were being lopped off, while his nose was being slit, while pieces of flesh were being cut from his body, and the bleeding wounds smeared with hot ashes; while his feet were roasting, while his limbs were being torn with hot splinters, while the flames leaped high about him, he shouted his death-song with a steady voice till his tormentors plucked out his tongue or brained him with a tomahawk. Yet this man, whose courage was unquestionable, was given to the dark and crooked ways which are the resort of the cowardly and weak. * * * He was never so happy as when at dead of night, he roused his sleeping enemies with an unearthly yell, and massacred them by the light of their burning homes. Cool and brave men who have heard that whoop, have left us a striking testimony of its nature; how that no number of reptitions could strip it of its terrors; how that, to the very last, at the sound of it the blood curdled, the heart ceased to beat and a strange paralysis seized upon the body." (Mc-Master's History of the United States.)

The Indians who inhabited our own valley have been described by a writer who made his observations at the time of the French and Indian War. "The men are tall, well made and active, not strong, but very dextrous with a rifle-barrelled gun, and their tomahawk, which they will throw with great certainty at any mark and at a great distance. The women are not so tall as the men, but well made and have many children, but had many more before spirits were introduced to them. They paint themselves in an odd manner, red, yellow and black intermixed. And the men have the outer rim of their ears cut, which only hangs by a bit, top and bottom, and have a tuft of hair left at the top of their heads which is dressed with feathers. Their watch coat is their chief clothing, which is a thick blanket thrown all around them, and they wear moccasins instead of shoes, which are deer-skin thrown around the ankle and foot. Their manner of carrying their infants is odd. They are laid on a board and tied on with broad bandages, with a piece to rest their feet on, and a board over their heads to keep the sun off, and are strung to the women's backs. These people have no notion of religion, or any sort of superior being, as I take them to be the most ignorant people as to the knowledge of the world and other things. In the day they were in our camp and in the night they go into their own, where they dance and make a most horrible noise."

These "children of nature" had singular aptness for learning all the most undesirable practices of their civilized neighbors and an equally singular inaptitude for learning anything that it was to their advantage to learn. But civilization puts its worst foot forward. The first whites with whom the red men came in contact were traders who were bent on cheating them, and taking advantage of their simplicity, and hunters and trappers who possessed the vices of civilization without many of its virtues. It was from these that the Indian took his first lessons, and by the time civilized whites, or the missionary reached him he had imbibed a fierce passion for "fire water," along, it may be, with a vindictive hatred of the white race which had cozened him. An old Cherokee chief informed an officer in the United States service that "he doubted the benefits to the red people of what they had learned from the whites; that before their fathers were acquainted with the whites, the red people needed but little and that little the Great Spirit gave them, the forest supplying them with food and raiment; that before their fathers were acquainted with

the white people, the red people never got drunk because they had nothing to make them drunk, and never committed theft because they had no temptation to do so. It was true, that when parties were out hunting and one party was unsuccessful and found the game of the successful party hung up, if they needed provision they took it; and this was not stealing—it was the law and the custom of the tribes. If they went to war they destroyed each other's property. This was done to weaken their enemy. Red people never swore because they had no words to express an oath. Red people would not cheat, because they had no temptation to commit fraud—they never told falsehoods because they had no temptation to tell lies. And as to religion, you go to your churches, sing loud, pray loud, and make great noise. The red people meet once a year, at the feast of new corn, extinguish all their fires and kindle up a new one, the smoke of which ascends to the Great Spirit as a grateful sacrifice. Now what better is your religion than ours? The white people have taught us to get drunk, to steal, to lie, to cheat and to swear; and if the knowledge of these vices, as you profess to hold them, and punish by your laws, is beneficial to the red people, we are benefitted by our acquaintance with you; if not, we are greatly injured by that acquaintance."

In point of fact, for over thirty years the Indians lived at peace with the settlers in the Hagerstown valley and committed no depredations upon their property other than now and then appropriating to their own use when they were on the war path, cattle and hogs that they encountered in their march.

The pioneer settlers of our valley were cut off from civilization by the Blue Ridge Mountains. They were cut off from all the conveniences of life, of which their brethren along the coast, having constant communication with the mother country, were never completely deprived. There was to them in case of need, no hope of effectual and timely help. They were surrounded by the savage red men, and had to struggle with nature for a livelihood. Wild mountain tracts separated them from their kind and kindred, and to the west of them lay the vast and unknown wilds which might have at any time, and did before many years, pour down upon them a destruction compared with which the invasion of Italy from the forests of the Danube was a merciful visitation of Providence. The settlers therefore had only themselves and their strong right arms to rely upon, and it made them an independent and hardy race, strong, healthy, moral and vigorous, untutored in evil and despising weakness and vice. The everyday comforts and conveniences which their descendants regard as the necessaries of life were unknown to them. It is a condition of society which has now disappeared. There are now no States of the Union as remote and inaccessible as the valley of the Antietam and Conococheague was in 1735. The settler of that time and for many succeeding years lived in houses built without a nail, because there were none to be had. He felled trees and cut them of the proper length, notched them near the ends and built a pen. After a height of seven or eight feet had been reached the end logs were made shorter and shorter until the side logs came together in an apex. A tree carefully selected was split up into boards and with these the roof was covered, being held in their places by heavy logs laid upon them, and the floor was formed of the same roughly made boards, smoothed as much as possible with a broad axe. A hole was cut for door and chimney place, a rough door was made and a chimney of stones and clay. The spaces between the logs were "chinked and daubed," a ladder was placed in position which gave access to the loft, or upper story and the residence was completed and ready for occupancy on the third day. In making the door-way, &c., wooden pins were used instead of nails. The men who cut the notches and fitted the logs together at the corner of the house occupied the posts of honor and were called the "corner men." The building of the house was not the work of the owner alone. He called in all his neighbors and when the work was completed, it was the occasion of a feast and frolic which generally lasted several days, and was only concluded when the guests and hosts had become exhausted.

Along with the house, the furniture was constructed. Holes were bored in the logs at proper places and pins were inserted which supported the shelves upon which utensils were kept. A fork was planted in the ground which supported two poles—the other ends resting between the logs of the side wall. This supported the bed. Pegs were driven in the sides of the house; upon these the wardrobe was displayed, and from them the rifle and powder horn were suspended. The dining table consisted of a large slab smoothed on one side with the broad axe, and supported on four legs, which were wedged into as many auger holes. Of china plates, cups and saucers and silver spoons he had none. Forks had no place in the domestic economy. A few of the wealthiest could boast of pewter plates and spoons, but the dinner plate of the average settler was of wood, which was indeed the material which most of his table furniture was made—namely, his bowls, trenchers and noggins. China plates would have been considered very undesirable, because in cutting food on them the hunting knife would be dulled. Gourds were more frequently used as drinking vessels.

With tea and coffee he had no acquaintance and his children grew up without ever tasting them. Milk, or water sweetened with maple sugar, washed down his meals of pork or bacon and hominy or mush. The latter was generally eaten with milk or sweetened water, bear's oil or gravy. Bacon was only used when there was no supply of bear steak, venison, wild turkey, raccoon or other game. Bread was an uncertain article of food and the settler's family might not taste it for months. It not unfrequently happened that after a hard year's work to raise a crop of corn for food for the winter, the settler would find when he came to harvest it in the autumn, that it had been already harvested by the squirrels and raccoons. In that case, his bill of fare for a whole year was greatly curtailed, and potatoes had to take the place of bread, hominy and mush. Even if the corn was secured, the process of converting it into meal was tedious and tiresome. It had to be done by beating it with a pestle in the huge wooden hominy mortars which formed a conspicuous article of furniture in every house, or else ground by hand between two rude millstones—a process almost as tedious as beating it with a pestle. When the corn was not yet hardened, it was sometimes grated through a home-made grater. The settler's family had frequently to wait for their breakfast until it could be procured with his rifle in the woods. The dress of the settler was as primitive as his dwelling and his furniture. The fashion of it was largely patterned after the attire of the Indian. He wore a hunting shirt of deer skin or home made linsey, confined around the waist by a belt. Appended to this shirt was a cape upon which some ornamentation of a rude type, was displayed. Breeches or leggins of deer skin, with deer skin moccasins confined to his feet by thongs or "whangs," completed his attire. Moccasins were easily made by means of a moccasin awl and thongs and were the only attainable covering for the feet. In dry weather the feet could be kept very comfortable, but when it was wet the deer-skin instantly became soaked and as a result of constant wet feet in winter the settlers suffered greatly from rheumatism. From the belt were suspended the tomahawk and scalping knife—those weapons of savage warfare which the whites were not slow in adopting—the powder-horn and other articles which might be needed in the field or forest. On his shoulder was carried the trusty rifle, which was the pioneer's inseparable companion, whether he went on a hunting expedition, or went into the field to plow or visited his neighbors. His wife and daughters were dressed in the "linsey petticoat and bedgown" and their only attempt at ornamentation was a homemade handerchief tied around the neck. They bore their part in the field and garden, besides performing their domestic duties, and had they been able to procure more beautiful garments, there would have been no occasion to wear them. Of shops and shopping they had no experience. The clothing of both men and women was the product of the rude domestic looms, or of the chase.

For many years there were no stores in the settlements, and the few necessaries which the settler required beyond those of his own production were brought on pack-horses across the mountain trail. Of vehicles there were none and had there been any there were no roads upon which they could be used. Upon pack-horses, then, the furs and peltries were carried to the towns nearer the seacoast—Baltimore after it grew to be a town, being the chief trading post; there they were exchanged for needed merchandise. Later, Hagerstown became an important distributing centre not only for what is now Washington County, but for a large section of the Valley of Virginia.

The principal article of trade which the early settler had to go across the mountain to procure was salt. This he must have at all hazards, and there was no possible method by which he could produce it. A number of men needing this commodity would associate and form a caravan to make the long and dreary journey to the seacoast. The bags which were to contain the salt were filled with feed for the horses on the journey down, and some of it was left at points along the way where it would be needed for the return trip, much in the same manner as travelers in the Arctic region cache provisions. Each horse was loaded with two bushels of salt. At the earliest period of the settlement it required the price of a good cow and calf to purchase a bushel of salt, and when filling the measure no one was allowed to walk heavily across the floor, for fear of shaking the salt down and getting too much into the measure.

Hunting was a serious occupation for the man of the backwoods, and not merely a pleasant diversion. For out of the woods he procured a good part of his food and his furs brought him in exchange his rifles, his ammunition, his salt and other necessaries. In the autumn he was eager to be off and was busy for many days before the time arrived in preparing his outfit. In this occupation he became skilful beyond the imagination of hunters who had no such material interest in the result of the chase. He studied the habits of animals with the assiduity of the naturalist, and practiced the stalking of the deer with the cunning and adroitness of the Indian himself. Several neighbors, when the time to begin the autumn hunt had finally arrived, would form a little company, and putting their provisions, their Indian meal, blankets and iron pot upon a pack horse, they sallied forth. Entering the forest, they selected the location for the hunting camp. This selection required no small exercise of judgment. It had to be in a secluded position, secure from the observation of Indians and game. It must be so situated as to be screened from the keen north winds. The hut was made of poles and covered with bark or slabs. The front, towards the south, was left open and the gipsy pot was suspended in front of it. At night the hunters brought in their game and slept with their feet towards the fire. They had to know intimately the habits of the deer and how their movements would be affected by the weather. In stormy weather they expected to find them in a different position from the ground they usually occupied when the weather was fair. They knew the points of the compass, and could guide themselves through the trackless forest by observing the bark of the trees and the moss, which grows more abundantly on the north side of the trunks. While in camp, the hunter rested from his labor on Sunday, but more from superstition than from religious motives. He was impressed with the belief that unless he did so his operations would be attended by ill-luck during the remainder of the week. Superstition was a prominent feature of the character of the simple folk. If an unfortunate person was bitten by a rattlesnake or a copper snake the reptile must be killed at all hazards, and was cut in sections about two inches long and laid on the wound to draw out the poison. The pieces were then gathered up and burned. Afterwards an application of boiled chestnut leaves was made. All remedies failed, however, when the rattlesnake got his fangs into any blood vessel which could quickly disseminate the poison throughout the body. It may be well imagined that casualties from rattlesnake bites were of frequent occurrence. Horses and cattle were also often killed by snakes. Hogs were more dangerous to the snakes than the snakes to the hogs. Charms and incantations were used in the treatment of many diseases, and candor compels us to admit that descendants of these people sometimes use them to this day. There were remedies in the garden and forest and field for all manner of diseases and the use of most of them was learned from the Indians. Walnut bark stripped upwards was used for one purpose and the same bark stripped from the tree by pulling it downwards was used to produce an entirely different result. The children suffered greatly from croup, which was called "bold hives" and they were treated with garlic or onion juice. Sweating was greatly practiced and bleeding would have been more frequently resorted to had it not been that there was no Dr. San Grado to administer this popular specific for all the ills to which flesh is heir.

A striking picture of the domestic life of the pioneers is given us by Mr. Samuel Kercheval who was the son of a pioneer and grew up just across the Potomac river from us, amidst the scenes he has described. The picture of the wedding which he gives bears every impress of truth and no one can doubt its accuracy.

"For a long time after the first settlement of this Country," writes Mr. Kercheval, "the inhabitants in general married very young. There was no distinction of rank and very little of fortune. On these accounts the first impression of love resulted in marriage, and a family establishment cost but a little labor and nothing else."

A description of a wedding from beginning to end, will serve to show the manners of our forefathers, and mark the grade of our civilization, which has succeeded to their rude state of society in the course of a few years. At an early period "the practice of celebrating the marriage at the house of a bride began, and it should seem with great propriety. She also has the choice of the priest to perform the ceremony. In the first years of the settlement of this County a wedding engaged the attention of a whole neighborhood, the frolic was eagerly anticipated by both old and young. This, is not to be wondered at when it is told that a wedding was almost the only gathering which was not accompanied with the labor of reaping, log-rolling, building a cabin, or planning some scout or campaign. On the morning of the wedding day, the groom and his attendants assembled at the house of his father, for the purpose of reaching the mansion of his bride by noon, which was the usual time for celebrating the nuptials, and which for certain must take place before dinner. Let the reader imagine an assemblage of people, without a store, tailor or mantuamaker, within an hundred miles, and an assemblage of horses, without a blacksmith or saddler within an equal distance. The gentlemen dressed in shoepacks, moccasons, leather breeches, leggins, and linsey hunting shirts, all home made. The ladies dressed in linsey petticoats and linsey or linen bed-gowns, coarse shoes, stockings, handkerchiefs, and buckskin gloves, if any; if there were any buckles, rings, buttons or ruffles, they were relics of old times, family pieces from parents or grand-parents. The horses were caparisoned with old saddles, bridles or halters, and pack-saddles, with a bag or blanket thrown over them—a rope or string as often constituted the girth as a piece of leather.

"The march in double file, was often interrupted by the narrowness and obstructions of our horse paths, as they were called, for we had no roads. These difficulties were often increased, sometimes by the good, and sometimes by the ill will of neighbors; by felling trees and tying grape vines across the way. Sometimes an ambuscade was formed by the wayside, and an unexpected discharge of several guns took place, so as to cover the wedding company with smoke. Let the reader imagine the scene that followed this discharge—the sudden spring of the horses, the shrieks of the girls, and the chivalric bustle of their partners to save them from falling. Sometimes, in spite of all that could be done to prevent it, some were thrown to the ground; if a wrist, elbow, or ankle happened to be sprained, it was tied with a handkerchief, and little more was thought or said about it.

"Another ceremony took place before the party reached the house of the bride, after the practice of making whiskey began, which was at an early period. When the party was about a mile from the place of its destination, two young men would single out to run for the bottle; the worse the path, the more logs, brush and deep hollows, the better, as these obstacles afforded an opportunity for the greater display of intrepidity and horsemanship. The English fox chase, in point of danger to the riders and their horses, was nothing to this race for the bottle. The start was announced by an Indian yell, when logs, brush, mudholes, hill and glen, were speedily passed by the rival ponies. The bottle was always filled for the occasion, so that there was no use for the judges for the first who reached the door was handed the prize and returned in triumph to the company announcing his victory over his rival by a shrill whoop.

"On approaching them he gave the bottle to the groom and his attendants at the head of the troop and then to each pair in succession, to the rear of the line, giving each a dram, and then putting the bottle in the bosom of his hunting shirt, he took his station in the company. The ceremony of the marriage preceded the dinner, which was a substantial backwoods feast of beef, pork, fowls and some times venison and bear meat, roasted and boiled, with plenty of potatoes, cabbage and other vegetables. During the dinner the greatest hilarity always prevailed, although the table might be a large slab of timber, hewed out with a broad-axe, supported by four sticks set in augur holes, and the furniture some old pewter dishes and plates, wooden bowls and trenchers. A few pewter spoons, much battered about the edges, were to be seen at some tables; the rest were made of horns. If knives were scarce, the deficiency was made up by the scalping knives, which were carried in sheaths suspended to the belt of the hunting shirt. After dinner the dancing commenced and generally lasted until the next morning. The figures of the dance were three and four handed reels or square sets and jigs. The commencement was always a square four, which was followed by what was called jigging it off, that is, two of the four would single out for a jig, and were followed by the remaining couples. The jigs were often accompanied by what was called cutting out, that is, when any of the parties became tired of the dance, on intimation, the place was supplied by some of the company, without any interruption of the dance; in this way a dance was often continued until the musician was heartily tired of his situation.

"Towards the latter part of the night, if any of the company through weariness attempted to conceal themselves for the purpose of sleeping, they were hunted up, paraded on the floor and the fiddler ordered to play "Hang out till Morning." About nine or ten o'clock a deputation of young ladies stole off the bride and put her to bed. In doing this, it frequently happened that they had to ascend a ladder instead of a pair of stairs, leading from the dining and ball room to the loft, the floor of which was made of clap boards lying loose without nails. This ascent, one might think, would put the bride and her attendants to the blush; but as the foot of the ladder was commonly behind the door, which was purposely open for the occasion, and its rounds at the inner ends were well hung with hunting shirts, petticoats and other articles of clothing, the candles being on the opposite side of the house, the exit of the bride was noticed but by a few. This done, a deputation of young men in like manner stole off the groom and placed him snugly by the side of his bride. The dance still continued, and if seats happened to be scarce, which was often the case, every young man, when not engaged in the dance, was obliged to offer his lap as a seat for one of the girls, and the offer was sure to be accepted. In the midst of this hilarity the bride and groom were not forgotten. Pretty late in the night some one would remind the company that the new couple might stand in need of some refreshment. Black Betty, which was the name of the bottle, was called for and sent up the ladder. But sometimes Black Betty did not go alone. I have many times seen as much bread, beef, pork and cabbage sent along with her as would afford a good meal for half a dozen hungry men. The young couple were compelled to eat more or less of whatever was offered them.

"In the course of the festivity, if anyone wanted to help himself to a dram and the young couple to a toast, he would call out, 'Where is Black Betty? I want to kiss her sweet lips.' Black Betty was soon handed to him, when, holding her up in his right hand he would say, 'Here's health to the groom, not forgetting myself, and here's to the bride, thumping luck and big children.' This, so far from being taken amiss, was considered as an expression of a very proper and friendly wish; for big children, especially sons, were of great importance as we were few in number and engaged in perpetual hostility with the Indians, the end of which no one could foresee. Indeed, many of them seemed to suppose that war was the natural state of man, and therefore did not anticipate any conclusion of it; every big son was therefore considered as a young soldier. But to return. It often happened that some neighbors or relations, not being asked to the wedding, took offense and the mode of revenge adopted by them on such occasions was that of cutting off the manes, foretops and tails of the horses of the wedding company.

"On returning to the infare, the order of procession and the race for Black Betty was the same as before. The feasting and dancing often lasted several days, at the end of which the whole company were so exhausted by loss of sleep, that several days rest were requisite to fit them to return to their ordinary labors.

"At these weddings the groomsmen wore embroidered white aprons and it was a part of their duty to serve up the wedding dinner and to protect the bride from having her shoe stolen from her foot while she was at dinner. If they failed, and the shoe was stolen, they had to pay a penalty for its redemption. This penalty was ordinarily a bottle of wine, and until the shoe was restored the bride was not permitted to dance. The same author already quoted gives this account of one of the wedding frolics: 'When the bride and groom were bedded, the young people were admitted into the room. A stocking, rolled into a ball, was given to the young females, who, one after the other would go to the foot of the bed, stand with their backs towards it and throw the stocking over their shoulders at the bride's head; and the first that succeeded in touching her cap or head was the first to be married. The young men then threw the stocking at the groom's head, in like manner with the like motive. Hence were the utmost eagerness and dexterity were used in throwing the stocking. This practice, as well as that of stealing the bride's shoe, was common to all the Germans.' "

Such were the simple and hardy folk by whom our beautiful valley was first peopled, and while for many years religion was almost a stranger to them, and children grew to manhood without seeing the inside of a Christian place of worship, they were a moral and just people. They dealt out rude justice among themselves before the regular forms of law were known among them, and it was proved that a healthy public sentiment which found ready and forcible expression when demanded, was more effectual in restraining vice than a regularly constituted constabulary.

CHAPTER II

THE pioneer who first ascended to the crest of South Mountain and cast his eyes over the valley stretching away to the foot of North Mountain, which bounds the landscape in front of him, viewed a picture to which no descriptive pen could do justice. If he had climbed up the eastern slope of the South Mountain, above the present site of Wolfsville, and through the gap until he came out at the Black Rocks, a spot, which in its romantic grandeur of ruggedness, has undergone no sort of change since that hour, he must have been indeed insensible if he did not pause here, spell-bound at the scene which presented itself to his eyes. If it appeared less beautiful to him than the promised land did to Moses as he viewed its vine clad hills and fertile valleys and streams of running water from the summit of Nebo, it was because he had not for forty years been traveling through hot sands and naked rocks.

He stood upon the summit of a cliff one hundred feet down perpendicular; and from the base of the cliff stretched a steep declivity, bearing no vegetation, because among the huge rocks piled and strewn and hurled against each other in some volcanic upheaval, there is no earth in which it can take root. To his right hand and to his left stretched away mountaintop after mountaintop covered with trees of great variety and form, and reaching north and south, to the limits of vision. Away to the west stretched a beautiful plain —the valley of the Antietam and the Conococheague, covered with waving grass six feet in height. Here and there the course of a stream was marked by trees which fringed each bank. He could have

seen columns of blue smoke ascending from clumps of trees which surrounded gushing limestone springs, marking the location of an Indian village. He might have seen, away off in the distance, where it breaks through the North Mountain on its way to the sea, a small portion of the Potomac or "Cohongoruton" river shimmering in the sun like molten silver. The awful silence around him would be broken only by the cry of the eagle over his head or the howl of the wolf, or perhaps the whoop of a savage, resting in a supposed secure possession of this beautiful hunting ground, unmindful of the wave of humanity which was slowly but surely coming upon him to wipe out almost the remembrance of his name and nation from the face of the country. He might have heard with prophetic ear

"The first low wash of waves, where soon
Shall roll a human sea."

Such was the valley of which Hagerstown is now the centre, in the early years of the eighteenth century. The mountains and the rugged western part of Washington County were covered with timber but the main valley was largely without trees, except along the water courses. We meet with frequent references, in contemporary writings, to the high grass which covered the country and the present state of the forest is ample proof of this fact. For it is rarely that an oak is seen in our forests, which are composed principally of oak and hickory, which has any appearance of being over a hundred years old. Speaking of the land just across the river from us in the valley of Virginia, a continuation of our own valley, Samuel Kercheval says that "at this period (1763, when the first settlement was made in the locality of which he was writing) timber was so scarce that settlers were compelled to cut small saplings to enclose their fields. The prairie produced grass five or six feet high and even our mountains and hills were covered with the sustenance of quadrupeds of every species. The pea vine grew abundantly on the hills and mountain lands, than which no species of vegetable production afforded finer and richer pasturage." This information Mr. Kercheval obtained from some of the original settlers.

Washington County is in general outline not unlike the State of Maryland. Its eastern boundary is the crest of the South Mountain, belonging to the Blue Ridge Range, which extends from Pennsylvania to Virginia, a distance of about thirty miles and separates Washington from Frederick County. Its northern boundary is Mason and Dixon's line, for a distance of forty-six miles. Its southern boundary line is the southern margin of the Potomac river, which separates it from Virginia and West Virginia and on the west it is separated from Allegany County, Maryland, by Sidling Hill Creek.

The main body of the County, known as Hagerstown Valley or a portion of Cumberland Valley, a northern continuation of the Valley of Virginia, is embraced between the North and South Mountains. The former crosses the County nearly parallel with South Mountain about fifteen miles distant. This valley is drained on the east side by the Antietam Creek, flowing a few miles from the base of South Mountain into the Potomac; towards the west, the valley is drained by the larger stream known as the Conococheague. The soil of nearly the whole of this valley is limestone of the best and most productive character. In the South-eastern portion of the County, there is a spur of the mountain known as Elk Ridge, running parallel with South Mountain a few miles distant from it and enclosing a valley known as Pleasant Valley, which has a freestone soil and is drained by Israel Creek. The southern extremity of Elk Ridge is the famous Maryland Heights, overlooking Harper's Ferry. Beyond the North Mountain are a series of ridges rising in undulations, enclosing between them here and there fertile valleys. The soil of the western portion of the County in the mountainous region, however, is mainly unproductive. Some of these ridges are known as East Ridge, Blair's Valley Mountain, Bare Pond, Forest Mountain, Haith Stone Mountain, Sidling Hill and Tonoloway Hill. In the main valley the scenery is that of a rich agricultural country displaying fertile fields, well cultivated farms, large barns and comfortable farm houses, with landscapes of magnificent beauty, having always the blue mountains for a background. The scenery of the County west of Clearspring is of romantic beauty. There is ridge after ridge, following each other like the waves of an ocean, covered with the deep verdure of the evergreens, and separated by narrow gorges and valleys, each with a rippling stream of crystal water breaking over its mossy stones and pebbly bottoms, and embowered amid trees of every variety of grace and beauty. The great industry of this magnificent County is agriculture, and the staple crops are, wheat and Indian corn. As a wheat growing county it ranks among the first in the Union. Oats, rye and barley are also grown, whilst the aggregate value of the clover seed, hay and poultry, and dairy products is enormous. Nearly all the fruits of the temperate zone are produced; apples in every variety and in vast quantity, grapes, small fruit and peaches. The last named fruit is grown in great perfection at a certain elevation on the western slope of South Mountain, where it seems to escape the damage from frost; and the cultivation of it in this region has assumed large proportions.

The mineral wealth consists of deposits of iron ore. Some traces of copper and antimony have been discovered in South Mountain, and of lignite in North Mountain. Cement of splendid quality is produced in the western part of the County, near Hancock, and in the southern part, opposite Shepherdstown. The principal manufactures are centered in Hagerstown. Here are made automobiles, paper, gloves, furniture, doors and sash, spokes and rims, iron tubes, hosiery, silk ribbons and underwear, and cigars. Transportation facilities are ample. Nine splendid turnpikes, penetrating to every district of the County, centre in Hagerstown. Railroads in seven different directions, besides electric roads to Williamsport and Frederick and into Pennsylvania afford competing lines to every important point in the County, and the Chesapeake and Ohio Canal meanders along the whole southwestern border for a distance of nearly a hundred miles affording an outlet to tidewater at the National Capital. The principal towns are Hagerstown, the County seat, Boonsboro, Williamsport, Clearspring, Hancock,

Sharpsburg, Keedysville, Smithsburg and Cave-town.

This county was a magnificent hunting ground for the Indians, who seem to have fought for it among themselves, and invaded it from the North and South just as the contending armies of the North and South did many years later. Of these contests there are only traditions. The Delawares from the North met here the Catawbas from the South, and the battles between the two were exceedingly sanguinary. Some of these battles took place just about the time when the white settlers first began to appear upon the scene. The settlers were upon terms of friendship with the Indians, and until a later period were entirely unmolested by them. About the year 1736, a bloody battle took place between these two hostile tribes at the mouth of the Antietam. At this point the Delawares, returning from one of their forays to the country of the Catawbas were overtaken by the latter. In the desperate battle which ensued every Delaware brave, with a single exception, had been killed and scalped and every Catawba warrior save one, had one or more scalps to exhibit after the victory. Like the Spartan who brought home the news of Thermopylae, this scalpless brave could not rest under the disgrace, and so he pursued the surviving and fugitive Delaware with the instinct and pertinacity of a blood hound for fully one hundred miles. The unfortunate fugitive was overtaken, slaughtered and scalped on the banks of the Susquehanna; the fair fame of the Catawba was retrieved, and he could return to his home.

There is a story of the early settlers connected with this bloody battle; whether founded on fact, or a mere product of the imagination, I cannot tell. The date of the battle given in this narrative is 1736. At that time, according to the tradition, there lived upon "Red Hill," an eminence near the Antietam about two miles from the scene of the battle and a short distance from Sharpsburg, a settler who was called Orlando, with his wife, Lauretta, a French woman, and their two children, a boy, Thomas, and a girl, Roseline. Hearing the sounds of the battle between the Delawares and Catawbas, the family fled to the side of South Mountain and there remained several days and nights, but partially protected from a severe storm by an overhanging rock. Whilst in this refuge a neighboring settler brought the news that it would be safe to return to their cabin. They did so, and found it undisturbed. It was not long before the boy, Thomas, was taken sick with a fever brought on by the exposure in the mountain and died. The mother, who had been delicately reared, soon followed her son to the grave and the health of the daughter was greatly impaired. In her grief and desolation she sought the society of the family of Peter Powles, living near the Belinda spring not far distant and in frequently passing it drank the waters and her health was restored. This was the first discovery of the medicinal property of that spring, which afterward became popular. But her restored health was not long enjoyed in peace. A Catawba chief fell in love with her and demanded her of Orlando for his wife. The proposal was rejected with horror but the savage was not to be defeated in his design. He frequently prowled around the cabin awaiting his opportunity, until one night he shot the father through an open window and bore off the unfortunate Rosaline to his wigwam. No news of her was ever afterwards received by her friends.

On the western side of the mouth of the Conococheague creek, after the settlement of Conococheague had begun, another bloody conflict took place between the Catawbas and Delawares, and the Delawares were again defeated. The surviving warrior this time took refuge in the house of Mr. Charles Friend, who lived very near the scene of the battle, and was by him protected from the ferocity of his pursuers. Just on the outskirts of Williamsport there was within the memory of many now living an Indian graveyard, which probably contained the bones of those who fell in that battle. Mr. John Tomlinson whose father lived on the Potomac, seven miles below the mouth of the Conococheague, informed Mr. Kercheval that he remembered when a child seven or eight years of age, seeing a party of Delawares pass his father's house, with a female Catawba prisoner, who had an infant child in her arms, and that it was said they intended to sacrifice her when they reached their towns.

There are remains of Indian settlements in various parts of the County. Around the great spring at Fountain Rock, the College of St. James, arrow heads and stone pipes and tomahawks have been very abundant, and a few years ago the author saw Indian skeletons exhumed in digging a cistern not far from this place. For many miles along the Potomac, Indian relics are abundant and in the neighborhood of Sharpsburg many mounds have been discovered. Some of these have been examined and found to contain bones, pottery and implements.

It is probable that a number of years before any regular, permanent settlement was made within the present limits of this County, the mountain had been crossed by hunters and trappers in quest of peltries and furs. The long grass afforded excellent pasturage for herds of deer, and the bears grew fat on the exuberant growth of those things they most esteemed for food. Wild turkeys were in great abundance, while the skulking wolf preyed upon anything he could overcome. The rocks and mountains were a refuge for the cat o'mounts and panthers, while the smaller folk, such as the opossum, the rabbit, the raccoon and squirrel, fairly swarmed. The two last were in such abundance that they frequently destroyed the settler's entire crop of Indian corn, leaving him without bread for a winter—a hardship which no one who has not experienced it can properly estimate, and for which he was only partially compensated by an abundant crop of potatoes. Some of the settlers came in the spring, bringing their families and no sufficient supply of either bread or vegetables, and they had to do without these necessaries of life until a crop could mature. In this case the sufferings of the family, and especially of the children, were very great. One who as a child had been deprived under these circumstances of all vegetable food for six weeks, wrote, "the lean venison and the breast of the wild turkeys, we were taught to call bread and the flesh of the bear was denominated meat." This artifice did not succeed very well; for after living in this way some time, we became sickly, the stomach seeming to be always empty and tormented with a sense of hunger. I remember how narrowly the children watched the growth of the potato tops, pumpkins and squash vines, hoping from day to day to get something to answer in the place of bread. How delicious was the taste of the young potatoes when we got them! What a jubilee when we were permitted to pull the young corn for roasting ears! Still more so when it had acquired sufficient hardness to be made into Jonny cakes by the aid of a tin grater. We then became healthy, vigorous and contented with our situation, poor as it was." *

In 1732 the attention of Charles, Lord Baltimore, had been directed to our valley and on the 2nd of March of that year he published the following advertisement offering inducements to settlers: "We being desirous to increase the number of honest people within our province of Maryland and willing to give suitable encouragement to such to come and reside therein, do offer the following terms:

"1st. That any person having a family, who shall within three years come and actually settle, with his or her family, on any of the back lands on the northern or western boundaries of our said province, not already taken up, between the rivers Potomack and Susquehanna, where, we are informed, there are several large bodies of fertile lands, fit for tillage, which may be seen without any expense, two hundred acres of said lands, in fee-simple, without paying any part of the forty shillings sterling, for every hundred acres, payable to us by the conditions of plantations, and without paying any quit rents in three years after the first settlement, and then paying four shillings sterling for every hundred acres to us, or our heirs, for every year after the expiration of the said three years.

"2nd. To allow to each single person, male or female not above the age of thirty, and not under fifteen, one hundred acres of the said lands, upon the same terms as mentioned in the preceding article.

"3rd. That we will concur in any reasonable method that shall be proposed, for the ease of such new-comers, in the payment of their taxes for some years and we doe assure all such that they shall be as well secured in their liberty and property, in Maryland, as any of his Majesty's subjects in any part of the British plantations, in America, without exception; and to the end all persons desirous to come into and reside in Maryland, may be assured that these terms will be justly and punctually performed on our part. We have hereunto set our hand and seal at arms." etc.

The class of people who were attracted to this valley by this advertisement, and still more by the richness of the soil and the salubrity of the air when they became known, were largely from Germany; but a great many of the largest land grants were to men of English descent from the eastern part of the State who were for many years the ruling people. But gradually their large estates became subdivided among their tenants and there are some instances of these men who spent their splendid estates and died poor. Many of our settlers came from Pennsylvania—some of them were Scotch-Irish and some German. A writer, in 1756, speaks of Conococheague as an Irish settlement and it is not improbable that the people who first built a block house and established a trading post at the mouth of the Conococheague were of that sturdy race of Scotch-Irish which "won the West" and contributed in no small degree to the triumph of the American arms in the war of Independence. The denial of religious freedom to the Presbyterians of Ulster in 1719 started the exodus from Ireland of the bravest and best subjects of the British crown. A steady stream of emigration to America set in, and continued for twenty-five years. Many of them landed at Philadelphia, and found their way to our valley. Many of them subsequently left it to take up their residence in the Kentucky wilderness, or among the dense and gloomy forests which covered the great valley of the Ohio. But many remained here, and in 1776 eagerly took up arms against their unnatural mother country which had cast them off. The descendants of many of them are among us now, and preserve the magnificent traits of character which distinguished their forefathers.

A considerable number of "Redemptioners" or Indented Servants also became citizens of the valley. Redemptioners were assisted emigrants—persons who wished to find a home in the colonies but not having sufficient money to pay their passage across the ocean sold themselves for a term of years for the necessary amount. The captain of the ship brought them over and then sold them for a sufficient sum to pay the passage. The practice was so extensively engaged in that it was regulated by an Act of Assembly passed in 1715, A servant being under fifteen years of age had to serve until he was twenty-two, if between fifteen and eighteen, seven years, if between eighteen and twenty-two, six years and five years if above twenty-five years of age. Usually their treatment was mild and they became freemen upon the expiration of the term of servitude; many of them, as well as of the convicts, became highly respected citizens, and the progenitors of influential families; and a few are mentioned as having become distinguished. One of the signers of the Declaration of Independence was a Redemptioner.

A much less desirable class of immigrants were the convicts. Thousands of the inmates of British prisons were transported to America and no less than three or four thousand found their way into Maryland each year. We cannot doubt that many of these were brought to our County. The people of the colony indeed protested loudly against this invasion and complained that it would introduce all the dreadful diseases then prevailing in the jails of England among our people. But they were powerless to remedy the evil. Pennsylvania did put a poll tax or tariff upon such importations and the Maryland Assembly attempted to do the same, but were met by an act of Parliament which authorized the business, and the Attorney General, afterwards Lord Mansfield, gave an opinion that the Colonial Assembly had no right to levy such a tax. The Colonial Assembly, however, persisted in collecting it, but it did not prevent the evil. Private parties made contracts with the government to ship these convicts to America and sell them for the benefit of the shippers. These transactions were a source of great profit to those engaged in them.

The first settlement made in this County was "Conococheague," a name which is spelled in contemporary documents and books in many entirely different and original ways. Governor Sharpe wrote it "Conogsgee" at one time and "Conegochegh" at another. In the Maryland Gazette it was generally printed as at present. General Braddock spelled it "Connogogee" and later in the same week "Conogogee." In fact, every writer spelled it to suit his own views and whenever he had another occasion to write the word forgot how he had spelled it the last time. The name and place were the occasion of a considerable amount of pleasantry in the United States Congress, as we shall see farther on. The settlement itself was situated on the Potomac, or Cohongoruton, as the Indians called that river above the mouth of the Shenandoah, at the mouth of Conococheague creek just about where the present town of Williamsport stands, or possibly on the opposite side of the creek. The first resident of the settlement who acquired a legal or documentary title to his land was Charles Friend, who in 1739 obtained a grant from the proprietor of 260 acres which he called "Sweed's Delight." It is situated on the west side of the Conococheague almost down to its mouth. Two years later, he was granted an additional tract of 25 acres adjoining "Sweed's Delight" which he called "Dear Bargain." It is likely that Friend had lived at this place five or six years before he received the deed for it. The descendants of this pioneer are still living in this county, a well known and highly respected family.

Conococheague soon became important as being the outpost of civilization in the province. A block house was built here, and it became a trading post of considerable importance. A mill was erected at an early date, and before many years regular communication was established and maintained with Frederick town, with which place it carried on trade. As early as 1163 supplies and provisions were dispatched eastward from this post. Later, as we shall see, it became more important as the terminus of the Potomac river boats plying between it and tidewater at George-town. A large magazine of stores was gathered here for General Braddock's army, and remained after his defeat. What finally became of it is not known, but it is not unlikely that when the inhab-itants of the settlement fled across the mountains, this supply fell into the hands of the Indians. It may well be supposed that there was a consider-able settlement at this point before any of the settlers took steps to secure legal titles to the lands they claimed.

In the year 1739, Jeremiah Jack obtained a grant for one hundred and seventy-five acres near "Sweed's Delight" which he called 'Jack's Bottom.' Before many years all the lands in this neighbor-hood had been claimed and taken up, until in 1780 Jacob Friend seems to have gotten the last, which he significantly called "None Left." This tract contained only three acres and a quarter. The second settlement of any consequence was "Long Meadows"—the settlement which took its name from the grant of 500 acres made to Thomas Cressap in 1739. This settlement was situated about three or four miles from Hagerstown, on the Leitersburg road, and being a most beautiful and fertile country, was speedily taken up—part of it, as elsewhere in the County, probably by land grabbers or speculators. Daniel Dulany, a non-resident, obtained in 1751 a grant adjoining Cressap's tract for 2131 acres which he called "Long Meadows Enlarged." The same name was given to a tract of 4163 acres granted to Henry Bouquet in 1765.

This Henry Bouquet never lived in this County. The centre of his tract is the farm for so many years owned by Mr. Frederick Wilms and the old house which he occupied and which is still standing, is one of the oldest and quaintest in the County. The owner of this great tract was a remark-able character in his time. He was born in 1719 at Rolle, a small town on the northern bank of Lake Geneva in Switzerland. In 1736, he entered the military service of the Dutch Republic. Short-ly afterwards he served as a petty officer in the army of the King of Sardinia and distinguished himself in the war with France. In 1756, the year after Braddock's defeat, Henry Bouquet sailed for America, and obtained a commission as colonel in the Royal service. His command was composed of the Swiss settlers of our valley and the Cum-berland Valley, of Pennsylvania, most of whom could not understand the English language. He was conspicuous in the campaigns around Fort Duquesne and he opened the road and established the route through Western Pennsylvania to Pitts-burg.

In his expedition against the Indians in 1764 Col. Bouquet had in his command two companies of Maryland troops, mostly volunteers from Wash-ington County. After the expedition the conduct of these troops was highly commended by their Colonel. One of the companies was officered by Captain, Wm. M. McClellan; Lieutenants, John Earl and James Dougherty; Ensigns, David Blair, John Moran, Edmund Moran; Sergeants, Joseph Hopewell and Henry Graybill. The officers of the other Maryland Company were: Captain, John Wolgomott; Lieutenant, Matthew Nicholas and Ensign John Blair. For his distinguished ser-vices in the Pontiac war, Col. Bouquet received a vote of thanks from the Colonial Assemblies of Virginia and Pennsylvania. After peace was es-tablished Bouquet determined to settle down in the Colonies and at that time he was naturalized in Pennsylvania, having two years previously obtained a grant of "Long Meadows Enlarged" from Lord Baltimore above referred to. The same year he received from the King a commission as Brigadier General and was ordered to Pensa-cola, when immediately upon his arrival he was smitten with yellow fever and died. Frederick Holdumand, his executor, was directed in his will to sell "Long Meadows Enlarged." This great tract of magnificent land contained in 1765 a saw mill, tan yard and a number of houses.

One of the oldest land grants in the County was "Chew's Farm" of 5000 acres granted to Samuel Chew, Jr., in 1763. "Chew's Farm" or "Chew's Manor," as it is frequently called, is in the south-ern part of the County lying near Mount Moriah

Church and Bakersville. As it was first granted, the lines ran across the river and into Virginia and so there was a re-survey. Connected with this grant is a tradition that the Proprietary Governor, (it must have been Ogle, for he was Governor at that time), was exploring this valley. The Governor and his party were overtaken by night near the house of Samuel Chew, and asked for hospitality. Mr. Chew received them courteously, but informed the party that his household was rather disarranged and they must make due allowances. During the night, the host became the father of a fine pair of twins who afterwards received the names of Samuel Chew and Bennett Chew. Shortly after the Governor returned to Annapolis, the patent deed for five thousand acres of land for Samuel Chew, Jr., one of the twins, was received.

One of the oldest buildings now in Washington County, is a substantial stone dwelling house in the same settlement with General Bouquet's property—the "Long Meadows" settlement. This stretch of country is the choicest portion of our valley and was eagerly taken up by settlers and speculators before any other settlements were made other than Conococheague. The building referred to is now owned by Daniel Scheller and stands upon a part of a tract known as "The Resurvey on Downin's Lot," which was owned for many years by William Ragan. The house was erected in 1750 by J. S. Downin, and a stone in the gable end bears this date and the initials of Downin. At one side of the chimney place an enclosed chamber was discovered which has been supposed to have been intended as a hiding place from Indians. But at the instance of the author it was carefully examined ,and then it was discovered that the fire place had been too enormously large for modern ideas and a wall had been built up to make it smaller. It is not far from this house that the remains of Cressap's Fort are still to be found.

The first town regularly laid out into lots in Washington County was Hagerstown. In December 16, 1739, Jonathan Hager obtained a patent for two hundred acres of land which he named "Hager's Choice." One of the boundary lines of this tract is described as beginning at "a bounded white oak standing on the side of a hill within fifty yards of said Hager's dwelling-house." This shows that Hager was residing near the present site of Hagerstown at that early date and that the

settlement at Hagerstown was nearly as early as those at Conococheague and Long Meadows. In 1753, he obtained a patent for another tract which he called "Hager's Delight." This latter tract contained 1780 acres. In 1762 the Proprietary gave him two other grants, one of a hundred and eighteen acres, which he called "Stony Batter," and another for twenty-four acres, which he called "Exchange." In 1763 he obtained three more grants, "Brightwell's Choice," "Addition to Stony Batter" and "Found it Out," containing respectively fifty, eighty and sixty-two acres. In 1765 he obtained "New Work," a tract of seven hundred and fourteen acres. He thus became possessed of two thousand four hundred and eighty-eight acres of magnificent land.

The main body of the town is situated on "New Work." Hager's dwelling was about two miles from the town on the Mercersburg road, on the farm recently owned by Henry Zeller. It was a large log house, a fine building in those days. There were two large log pens far enough apart to constitute a hall. Near the house was a burial vault, and in it the body of Hager was laid after his tragic death, but it was afterwards removed to the graveyard of Zion Church, in Hagerstown, where his ashes now lie.

The Southwestern portion of Hagerstown is upon "The Land of Prospect" and was added to the town by Jacob Rohrer who obtained the grant. This Rohrer was the progenitor of a large and influential family in this County. At the period of Hager's settlement in the valley almost the whole country was unoccupied and he probably had his choice. It is reasonable, therefore, to suppose that there was some especial attraction to the particular spot which he made his home—either in the character of soil, the beautiful prospect or the neighborhood of several gushing springs. It is probable that this latter consideration influenced most of the early settlers. Of this important settlement, which developed into the present beautiful town, the seat of the County, and of its founder, more will be said in a subsequent chapter.

Among the early settlers, few invested so largely in land as Joseph Chapline. We have at hand the records of no less than nineteen different grants from the Proprietary, transferring to him 15,400 acres. The greater part of this land was in the neighborhood of Sharpsburg, although some of it was in Pleasant Valley. The Antietam Iron Works was included in his grant for 6352 acres which he called "Little I Thought It." On July 9, 1763, Chapline laid out on his tract "Joe's Lot," the town of Sharpsburg in lots and named it in honor of Governor Horatio Sharpe, who was at that time the Proprietor's active representative at Annapolis. Chapline, who came from England —along with two brothers, Moses and James, must have been one of the earliest settlers in the County, for he had a grant of land in 1753, about eighteen years after the very first settlement. In 1728 he had settled in Boston. He was a distinguished citizen of the County and was several times a member of the Assembly. He was a soldier in the French and Indian war, and the muster roll of his company, in which he was lieutenant, was recently discovered in his house by John P. Smith who preserves it. His farm, Mt. Pleasant, was on the Potomac river about two miles from Sharpsburg, and there in a private graveyard his body lies buried.*

When Chapline laid out Sharpsburg, which is next to Hagerstown the oldest town in the County, there were four houses in it. One was a log house used for years as an Indian trading post, another stood for the present Methodist Church and was torn down in late years. The other two are still standing—the log house, now brick cased, lately owned by Samuel Michael, and a portion of the house owned by the heirs of Jacob Miller. Living near Welsh Run at this time was a Welsh minister named William Williams. He was a Presbyterian missionary to Virginia and after the death of his wife he emigrated to America and settled in Frederick County, Virginia. Here he was indicted and tried for performing a marriage ceremony, which under the laws of the

Province could only be done by a clergyman of the established church. He then came to Maryland with his three daughters. One of them, Ruhannah, married Chapline; the second, Jane, married William Price, a lawyer in Hagerstown, after it was made the county seat; and the third, Sarah, married Colonel Chambers, the founder of the town of Chambersburg, Pa. All three were runaway matches. From Joseph Chapline and his wife, Ruhannah, who had nine children, Mrs. Julia Alvey, the wife of Hon. Richard H. Alvey, formerly Chief Justice of Maryland, is descended on her father's side, and she has a curious ring which her father, Dr. Hays, inherited. It is inscribed,

"William Williams is my name
Christ and His glory is my aim."

William Williams' wife owned a large property in Caermathonshire, Wales, and her daughter, Mrs. Chambers, went to Wales and obtained her portion. The other two daughters never did.

Joseph Chapline's oldest son, Joseph, inherited the Mt. Pleasant estate. He was a man of great consequence and an officer in the Revolutionary War—leading a large body of volunteers to the army. He died at Mt. Pleasant in September, 1821, aged 75 years.

A log church was built in fulfilment of the condition of a deed from Chapline, and was used by the congregation until the battle of Antietam in 1862, when it was so shattered by Federal shells that it had to be taken down and a new one built. Before its destruction, it was used as a hospital by the Federal troops. In 1866, a new church was built, but not upon the same lot. In 1775, a Reformed Church was built in Sharpsburg, and

---

*In 1768 Joseph Chapline and Ruhannah Chapline his wife, executed the following deed: "This Indenture, made this 5th day of March, 1768, between Joseph Chapline of Frederick County, Province of Maryland, on one part, and Christopher Cruss, Matthias Need, Nicholas Sam and William Hawker, vestrymen and church wardens of the Lutheran Church in the town of Sharpsburg, in the County aforesaid, of the other part:

Witnesseth, that the said Joseph Chapline, for and in consideration of the religious regard he hath and beareth to the said Lutheran Church, and also for the better support and maintenance of the said Church, hath given, granted, aliened, and enfeoffed and confirmed and by these presents doth give, grant, alien and enfeoff and confirm to the said Christopher Cruss, Matthias Need, Nicholas Sam, and William Hawker, vestrymen and church wardens, and their

successors, members of the above church, for the use of the Congregation that do resort thereto, one lot or portion of ground, No. 149, containing one hundred and fifty-four feet in breadth and two hundred and six foot in length with all profits, advantages and appurtenances to the said lot or portion of ground belonging or appertaining, to have and to hold to them the said Christopher Cruss, Matthias Need, Nicholas Sam and Wm. Hawker, vestrymen and church wardens and to their successors forever to them and to their own use, and to no other use, intent or purpose whatever, yielding and paying to the said Joseph Chapline, his heirs and assigns, one pepper corn, if demanded, on the 9th day of July, yearly. And if the above named vestry do not build a church on said lot in a term of seven years, then the above lot to revert to the said Joseph Chapline, his heirs and assigns."

George Washington Monument. The First Ever Erected to His Memory, and was Built by Citizens of Boonsboro, in 1827.

then no others for many years. The Methodists organized a congregation here in 1811 and the Episcopalians in 1818, by the Rev. Benj. Allen, of Shepherdstown. Christopher Cruss, one of the grantees in the deed given above, was a German chemist, and among the first persons who became citizens of the new town. It is claimed that he was interested with Rumsey in his steamboat enterprise, the trial of which took place in the Potomac River, near Sharpsburg. There is a mill now standing near Sharpsburg, owned by Jacob A. Myers, which was built in 1783 and the dwelling near it forty years earlier. This was the home of Christian Orndorff the father-in-law of Jonathan Hager, Jr. It will thus be seen at what an early period the water power of the Antietam was utilized.

Another proof of the rapidity with which the lands of the valley were "taken up" after the tide of emigration began to set this way, is the early date of the settlements in the Western part of the County and notably the one at Green Spring. The most conspicuous person connected with this settlement was Lancelot Jacques. He was a French Huguenot who came to America as a refugee. He fell in with Thomas Johnson, then a rich provincial of Frederick County, a leading citizen of Maryland, a friend of Washington, and afterwards the first Governor of the State of Maryland. Jacques, soon after his arrival in this country, became associated with Johnson in many enterprises. Together they became patentees of large tracts of land with a view, not merely of speculating, but of improving the country and developing its resources. With this view they obtained a large grant of land in what is now Frederick County, and upon it constructed and operated the Catoctin Furnace. Later, they obtained a patent for fifteen thousand acres at Indian Spring, and here Jacques came to reside not far from Fort Frederick, and here his house still stands. The discovery of excellent iron ore suggested a smelting furnace. The pig iron manufactured in this furnace was pushed down the river on flat boats by a crew of trusty negroes owned by Jacques.*

---

*The following is the deed from Lord Baltimore conveying the Furnace property to Johnson and Jacques, which is here given nearly in full as showing this early enterprize and as also showing the character of most of the land grants in our Valley:

Maryland, ss.—Frederick, Absolute Lord Proprietary of Maryland and Avalon Lord Baron of Baltimore, &c.

Whereas: Lancelot Jacques and Thomas Johnson, Jun., of the City of Annapolis, have obtained out of our High Court of Chancery within our said Province, our writ of ad quod damnum, directed to the Sheriff of Frederick County, commanding him by the oath of Twelve honest and lawful men of his county, by whom the truth of the matter might be better known, he should diligently enquire if it would be to the Damage of us or others if we should grant unto the said Lancelot Jacques and Thomas Johnson, Jun., one hundred acres of land lying on a run of water called Green Spring Run, otherwise called Lick Run, in the County aforesaid, about two miles below Fort Frederick, as might be most convenient for setting up a Forge Mill and other conveniences, as shall be necessary for carrying on an Iron Work, and if it should be to the Damage and Prejudice of us and others, then to what Damage and Prejudice of us, and what Damage and Prejudice of others and of whom and in what manner and how and of what value, the same land was then before any other improvements of the said one hundred acres of land, and who were the possessors of the said one hundred acres of land, and who had the Fee Simple thereof, and what lands and Tenements remained to the Possessors over and above the said One Hundred Acres of Land, and if the said Land remaining to the Possessors over and above the said One Hundred Acres will suffice to uphold their Manor, vizt. the sixth part of their Manor allotted them by the condition of Plantation for the Demesne as before the alienation aforesaid in default of the present possession more than was wont might not be charged and grieved, and that the Inquisition thereupon openly and distinctly made to us in our High Court of Chancery under his seal and seals of them by whom it was made he should without delay send and whereas the aforesaid Sheriff, at the instance and request of the above named Lancelot Jacques and Thomas Johnson, Junr., hath returned into our said Court a certain inquisition Indented and taken in Frederick County on the said Run of Water called Green Spring Run, otherwise called Lick Run, on the 23rd day of December in the year of our Lord 1765, by the oath of twelve honest and lawful Men of the County, who upon their oath did say that if we should grant unto the said Lancelot Jacques and Thomas Johnson, Jun., the said One Hundred Acres of Land lying on the said Run of Water, beginning at a locust post set up near the south easternmost corner of the Coal House (here follow the courses and distances) containing One Hundred Acres, and which is fit and convenient for building an Iron Work for running of Pigg Iron, it would not be to the damage of us, the said One Hundred Acres or any part thereof not being a Manor, or any part of a Manor, and that the same One Hundred Acres is of the value of One Hundred Pounds current money without any further Improvement and no more that the Possession and Fee Simple of the said One Hundred Acres is in the said Lancelot Jacques and Thomas Johnson, Jun., in undivided Moietys as Tenants in Common

In 1776 Johnson and Jacques dissolved partnership, the latter retaining as his portion of the property, the Green Spring Furnace estate. In addition to his other enterprises, Jacques acted as agent for a number of English owners of Maryland plantations, and indeed it was in this capacity that he first came to America. His descendants have in their possession some of his account books of the plantations.

It is somewhat remarkable that Boonsboro was not settled earlier than it was, for it is a beautiful and attractive situation, and it is likely that most of the settlers from the eastern part of the State came to the valley through the gap, where the National road now passes. Here, at the foot of the mountain, Boonsboro lies. The land upon which the town is situated and that all around it, was granted to George and William Boone in about 1774. These men lived in Berks County, Pa. The latter came to his property in Maryland and resided there until his death in 1798. He and his wife are both buried in the Reformed Churchyard in the village. His wife, Susanna, survived him forty-six years, dying in 1844 at the age of eighty-eight years. The daughter of this couple, Sarah Boone, died at Keedysville in September 1874. The town did not grow rapidly. In 1796 there were only five houses and in 1829, Henry Nyman and Betebanner bought the Boone property, and laid out the town in lots. At that time there were only twenty-nine houses in the place.

The following is an account of a journey by Wm. Eddes, an Englishman, who was at the time Commissioner of the Land Office at Annapolis, taken from his Letters:

Annapolis, Sep. 7th, 1772.

"I am just returned from an excursion to the frontiers of this province, in which my curiosity was highly gratified. It is impossible to conceive a more rich and fertile country than I have lately traversed; and when it becomes populous in proportion to its extent, Frederick County will, at least, be equal to the most desirable establishment on this side of the Atlantic.

"In the back settlements, where the inhabitants are thinly scattered, the face of the country, even at this luxuriant season of the year, exhibited in many places a dreary appearance. Lands, to a very considerable extent, are taken up by persons who, looking to futurity for greater advantages, are content to clear gradually some portions of their domains for immediate subsistence. Not having the means to fell and carry their lumber away, they make a deep incision with an axe entirely round each trunk, at the distance of about four feet from the ground, which occasions the leaves almost instantly to wither; and before the total decay of the tree, Indian corn may be cultivated to great advantage, amidst the immense trunks that fill the dreary forest.

"To have the idea of winter impressed on the mind, from external appearances, at the time when nature is fainting beneath the intense heat

and on part of two Tracts of Land, the one called the Resurvey on Green Spring, the other called Kindness, and that there remains to the said Lancelot Jacques and Thomas Johnson, Jun., over and above the said One Hundred Acres of Land well and sufficient to uphold their Manors, vizt., the sixth part of their respective Manors allotted to them by the conditions of Plantations:—and whereas the said Lancelot Jacques and Thomas Johnson Jr., hath given their respective Manors allotted them by the Conditions of Plantations and Whereas the said Lancelot Jaques and Thomas Johnson, Jun., hath given sufficient security to us that they the said Lancelot Jaques and Thomas Johnson, Jun., shall begin to prosecute and finish the building a Forge Mill and other conveniences on the said Land within the time limited in and by the Act of Assembly—Now Know Ye, that we, for and in consideration of the premises, do grant unto said Lancelot Jaques and Thomas Johnson, Jun., the said One Hundred Acres of Land contained within the lines aforesaid, with all privileges, rights, profits, and advantages thereto belonging, Royal Mines excepted with free egress and regress through any mans Land next adjoining to the said

Forge Mill to have and to hold said one undivided moiety of the said 100 Acres of Land to the said Lancelot Jaques and his heirs and assigns forever and to have and to hold the other undivided moiety thereof to him the said Thomas Johnson, Jun., his heirs and assigns forever, as Tenants in Common, and not in Joint Tenancy to be holden of us as of our Manor of Conogocheague yielding and paying unto us and our heirs and successors the same Rents, Fines and Services as are reserved, due and payable unto us for the said One Hundred Acres of Land, anything in these presents to the contrary notwithstanding. Witness our Trusty and well beloved Horatio Sharpe, Esq., Governor and Commander in Chief in and over the Province aforesaid this 11th day of April in the seventeenth year of our Dominion Anno Domini 1768." This grant is countersigned on the margin by Horatio Sharpe; and appended to it by a ribbon is a seal nearly four inches in diameter. The impression is made upon wax enclosed between two sheets of paper. Upon one side the seal is the familiar seal of the Province—representing Agriculture and Fisheries—the other side has the Knightly Seal.

of an autumnal sun, is, I am inclined to believe, peculiar to this country. In some districts, far as the eye could extend, the leafless trees of an astonishing magnitude crowded on the sight; the creeping ivy only denoting vegetation; at the same time, the face of the earth, was covered with golden crops, which promised, "richly to repay the anxious toil." The habitations of the planters, in this remote district of the province, are in general of a rude construction; the timber with which they frame their dwellings seldom undergoing the operation of any tool except the axe. An apartment to sleep in, and another for domestic purposes, with a contiguous store-house, and conveniences for their live-stock, at present gratify their utmost ambition. Their method of living perfectly corresponds with their exterior appearance. Indian corn, beaten in a mortar, and afterwards baked or boiled, forms a dish which is the principal subsistence of the indigent planter, and is even much liked by persons of the superior class. This, when properly prepared, is called homony,, and when salt beef, pork, or bacon is added, no complaints are made respecting their fare.·

"Throughout the whole of this province fruit is not only plentiful, but excellent in various kinds. There are few plantations unprovided with an apple and a peach orchard; the peach trees are all standards, and without the assistance of art, frequently produce fruit of an exquisite flavor.

"In the woods, I often meet with vines, twining round trees of different nominations; and have gathered from them grapes of a tolerable size, and not unpleasant to the palate. In process of time, when the colonists are enabled to pay attention to their natural advantages, they will, assuredly, possess all the superfluities of life, without the necessity of recurring to foreign assistance. Even sugar, of a tolerable quality they will be able to manufacture without application to the British Islands. A planter, at whose house I partook of some refreshments produced a quantity of that capital luxury, the grain of which was tolerable, and the taste not disagreeable. This, he assured me, was the produce of his own possessions. extracted by incision, from a tree, great numbers of which grow throughout the interior regions of the American provinces, (the maple tree).The simple process of boiling brought the liquid to a proper consistency; and he was persuaded, whenever more important concerns would

permit a necessary attention to this article, the inhabitants of the British colonies would be amply supplied from their own inexhaustible resources.

"About thirty miles west of Fredericktown, I passed through a settlement which is making quick advances to perfection. A German adventurer, whose name is Hagar, purchased a considerable tract of land in this neighborhood, and with much discernment and foresight, determined to give encouragement to traders, and to erect proper habitations for the stowage of goods, for supply of the adjacent country. His plan succeeded; he has lived to behold a multitude of inhabitants of lands, which he remembered unoccupied; and he has seen erected in places, appropriated by him for that purpose, more than an hundred comfortable edifices, to which the name of Hagar's Town is given, in honour of the intelligent founder."

Capt. Jonathan Hager arrived in America about the year 1730 and pushed on to the "back country" of the Province of Maryland. The date of his arrival at his future home is not accurately known, but it must have been shortly after the very first settlement of Conococheague and the location of Col. Cressap at Long Meadows. In 1739, when Hager obtained his first deed from Lord Baltimore, that conveying to him the tract of two hundred acres which he called "Hagar's Choice," he was living in a house which had already been built upon it. It contained an arched cellar, which was the refuge of Mr. Hager and his family during the Indian war.

The first of the large and influential family of Poffenbergers who came to this County was John Poffenberger, who arrived here from Pennsylvania in 1760, and bought a farm on the road leading from the Hagerstown and Sharpsburg turnpike to Keedysville, near a small hamlet called Smoketown.

Unlike the Hagerstown Valley, Pleasant Valley was covered with a dense and almost impenetrable·forest and the early settlers had hard work to bring their lands under cultivation. This woods was alive with wolves and other beasts of prey which destroyed the domestic animals of the settlers. The valley was settled by the ancestors of many of the principal families which still live in it—the Botelers, Clagetts, Grimms, Browns and Rohrers. Among the first was Thomas Crampton, who was born on the ocean in 1735, as his mother was on her way to this country. His father had just died and requested that the infant to be born should be named Thomas, whether it should be a boy or a girl. The family settled in Prince George's county, and Thomas Crampton came to Pleasant Valley before 1759. Through this wilderness was cut a road which led from the old pack horse ford below Shepherdstown, through Crampton's Gap and on to Fredericktown. The first enterprise of the settlers in the valley was to clear up the forest and plant tobacco. The tobacco was packed in hogsheads, to which shafts were fixed, and they were wheeled along this road to market. Old Mr. Crampton died Thursday morning, May 20, 1819, at the age of 84 years.

In 1777 a considerable body of immigrants arrived in the County, from a very unexpected quarter. These were a portion of Gen. Burgoyne's army, which had surrendered at Saratoga that year. They were soon assimilated by the population and became good and useful citizens. Among these was a young Irishman, who had been pressed into the British Army. His name was John Whistler. A short time after this surrender, he came to the neighborhood of Hagerstown, and remained there for some time. He married an English lady, named Bishop. He was afterwards made a Sergeant and Sergeant-Major of Infantry in the Continental Army and on the raising of a Battalion of Levies (volunteers) in that section of the State in 1791, he was appointed Adjutant of Major Henry Gaither's Battalion in Lt. Col. Wm. Darke's Regiment for frontier defence. He was wounded in the battle under Maj. Genl. St. Clair, with Indians on the Miami, November 1791. He was afterwards made Ensign, Lieutenant, Quartermaster, and Captain of the Regular Army; was Brevet Major and died while serving as military storekeeper at Belle Fontaine, near St. Louis, Mo., in 1827. From him descended all the Whistler family in this country. Col. George Whistler, a distinguished civil engineer, in Russia, was one of his sons. He also left several sons in the U. S. Army. Among his descendants is Whistler the distinguished painter.

Another of these immigrants was Major Alexander Monroe, of Scotland, who settled in Washington County and died here November 6, 1797, greatly beloved. He was buried in the Episcopal graveyard with the honors of war, in the presence of a great concourse of people—the Rev. George Bower conducting the services.

In September, 1784, there arrived at Funkstown a family of immigrants who excited more than ordinary interest. They were Dr. Christian Boerstler, his wife and six children accompanied by a considerable body of Germans. Dr. Boerstler was born January 29, 1749, in the Dukedom of Duex Ponts, a portion of the Kingdom of Bavaria. Owing to the tyranny of the German Princes he determined to emigrate to America. Accordingly, in 1784, he demanded passports. The secretary of foreign relations of his native country endeavored to dissuade him from his project. He represented to him the long and dangerous journey he was undertaking, and the wild and unsettled country to which he was going, and offered him a high position under the Government. But the Doctor was not to be turned from his purpose, and after the passports were obtained, he found himself at the head of seventy families of emigrants as their leader and pioneer. On his way to his ship he met with his Prince, who inquired where he was going with all those people. Boerstler replied that he was going to America to be free. "Under your reign we are slaves and if you continue your oppressions much longer you will have no subjects to rule." The party went in boats from the Kline to Rotterdam and there took ship for Baltimore. But before doing so a narrow escape was made from being forced on a slave ship bound for Batavia. When Dr. Boerstler landed in Baltimore he had but a single shilling in his possession and owed a guinea on the ship. He found means, however, to make his way to Washington County and settled in Funkstown. He soon became one of the leading citizens of the County, took a prominent part in the political movements which resulted in the adoption of the Constitution of the United States. He secured the support of the German people to this measure by a series of vigorous essays over the signature of "Volksfreund." During the Whiskey Insurrection he bore an important part in the support of the Government. He took an active interest in agriculture and wrote many articles on the importance of the cultivation of clover. He was largely instrumental in the early introduction of that crop among the farmers of Washington County. Raising bees was also a matter which greatly interested him and he wrote much upon the subject. It was he who furnished for many years the reading matter for the German Almanac published in Hagerstown. Col. Boerstler, who became well known in the war of 1812 was his son. Dr. Boerstler died in Funkstown, March 11, 1833, in the eighty-fifth year of his age.

The following extract from a life of the Rev. Michael Schlatter gives a picture of the valley at an early date and refers to another early settlement in Washington county. It is of interest, notwithstanding the numerous inaccuracies contained in it:

"His course from Frederick was nearly in a North line, to what is now Burkittsville, and thence diverging to nearly east, he crossed the mountain through what is now, and always has been known as "Crampton's Gap," thence by way of Rohrersville in Pleasant Valley, and Keedysville on the Antietam, about three miles southwest from where Boonsboro now stands; thence in a westerly direction to the settlements on the Conogocheague, about seven or eight miles west of Hagerstown; and the place where he preached at the time, must have been somewhere in the vicinity of what is now "Saint Paul's Church," in the vicinity of Clearspring, which is the oldest congregation in that country. Here the first settlement in the county was made, the first settlers being Germans, and members of the Reformed and Lutheran churches; as Reformed families I can name the Kershners, Seiberts, Sellers, and Prices. They settled on the Conococheague, because in 't they found good timber for building and other uses, whilst the rest of the valley was destitute of timber, and only covered with *scrub-oak* and *hazle-bushes*. Near Clearspring and on the Potomac, are still to be seen the remains of a fort they built, and in which they kept their families when the Indians became troublesome. This was afterwards rebuilt by Gen. Braddock and was then called Fort Frederick and is still known by that name.* The country was then destitute of roads and the way pursued by Mr. Schlatter was simply a horse path or trail, though afterwards laid out into a public road, and so used until some forty or fifty years ago as the great highway to the West. Who the honest Swiss was, I cannot tell but presume he must have been one of the families I have named. (Letter from Lewis M. Harbaugh, Esq., of Hagerstown, Md., dated Dec. 13, 1856.)

"On the 7th of June 1748, I continued forty miles farther to Monocacy in the province of Maryland, where on the 11th, in Fredericktown, a newly laid out town, I preached a preparatory sermon in the schoolhouse; and on the same day, in company with an elder of this congregation, who of his own free will offered to accompany me through Virginia, I continued my journey thirty-four miles farther to Conochocheague, crossing the so-called Blue Mountains, so that we did not arrive in Connogocheague till two o'clock in the morning of the 9th, when we came to the house of an honest Swiss, and gratefully enjoyed a very pleasant rest. I preached there yet on the same day. This congregation, lying to the north from Maryland, and hence belonging still to Pennsylvania, might be served by the ministry at Monocacy. Here in this region there are very fruitful fields for grain and pasture; they produce Turkish corn almost without any manure, among which are stalks ten and more feet long; and the grass is exceedingly fine. In this neighborhood there are still many Indians, who are well disposed and very obliging, and are not disinclined toward Christians, when they are not made drunk by strong drink. After the sermon, we left and passed on ten miles farther toward the Potomac river, which is at this place one mile wide, from which also we had a fine view of the place, where the Connogocheague stream falls into this river. Here is a boundary at once between Pennsylvania and Virginia and between Maryland and Virginia. This evening we journeyed fifteen miles without having seen either a house or a human being; but we saw deer in droves."

"The point where we crossed the Potomac at the mouth of the Connogocheague is where Williamsport now stands, which is next to the oldest town in the county. Here it was then supposed the line, run along afterward (in 1761) by Mason and Dixon, would strike the Potomac."

(Letter of Lewis M. Harbaugh, Esq., of Hagerstown, Md., December 13, 1856.)

The Potomac is not ordinarily a mile wide—it may have been swollen by rains at the time. "Some of the early settlers in Martinsburg and vicinity say that they remember when the river spread itself very wide, so that when high, it might with truth be said, it was about a mile wide."

(Letter from Rev. J. G. Wolf.)

---

*This of course is incorrect.

Printed in the USA
CPSIA information can be obtained
at www.ICGtesting.com
LVHW010510241223
767241LV00006B/641